# The Kaleidoscope Leader

*Trudy Jean Evans*

*The Kaleidoscope Leader*

Copyright © 2015 Trudy Jean Evans. All rights reserved. No part of this book may be reproduced or retransmitted in any form or by any means without the written permission of the publisher.

Published by Wheatmark®
2030 East Speedway Boulevard, Suite 106
Tucson, Arizona 85719
United States of America
www.wheatmark.com

ISBN: 978-1-62787-127-3 (paperback)
ISBN: 978-1-62787-128-0 (ebook)
LCCN: 2014935500

rev202001

# Contents

| | |
|---|---:|
| *Introduction* | 1 |

## *The Six Styles of Leadership*

| | |
|---|---:|
| The Solutions-Based Leader | 7 |
| The Servant-Centered Leader | 9 |
| The Process-Driven Leader | 11 |
| The Financially-Focused Leader | 15 |
| The Visionary Leader | 17 |
| The Charismatic Leader | 19 |
| In Closing | 21 |

## II
## *The Six Beliefs of a Kaleidoscope Leader*

| | |
|---|---:|
| Put Others First | 27 |
| Take Ownership | 39 |
| Foster an Optimistic Attitude | 53 |
| Drive Results Through the Details | 67 |
| Inspire Others | 81 |
| Practice Lifelong Learning | 95 |
| *Conclusion* | 109 |

# Introduction

A kaleidoscope is a circle of mirrors containing loose, colored objects, such as beads or pebbles and bits of glass. As the viewer looks into one end, light entering the other end creates a colorful pattern due to the reflection off the mirrors.

Kaleidoscope leaders are individuals who embrace a multitude of leadership techniques to be successful. As they look within, their methods of leading change due to the reflection they see in others. This is a book about how leaders can reach their peak through the utilization of a variety of skills, talents, and behaviors to guide themselves and others to greatness.

All of us are made up of many facets. As we blend these facets together, we change the way we act. The circumstances we face cause us to tap into our creativity, knowledge, and wisdom, which in turn directs us to different outcomes. It is this very blend of who we are that shapes a kaleidoscope leader.

This book presents the six styles of leadership and examines the importance of each one—how the effectiveness of one style can produce greatness, but when used in excess, can also become an impediment. You will be introduced to the six beliefs of a kaleidoscope leader and how this individual incorporates all six styles to create a leadership life of joy, abundance, satisfaction, and triumph.

Based on the philosophy that an individual's success is predicated on the success of others, *The Kaleidoscope Leader* will teach you how you can become a leader others will want to follow.

# I
## *The Six Styles of Leadership*

Before being introduced to the kaleidoscope leader, let's examine six basic styles of leadership. They are:
1. The Solutions-Based Leader
2. The Servant-Centered Leader
3. The Process-Driven Leader
4. The Financially-Focused Leader
5. The Visionary Leader
6. The Charismatic Leader

Every leader typically falls predominately into at least two of these categories. The more emotionally intelligent they are, the more they tap into the other styles. The kaleidoscope leader is the perfect blend of all six, knowing when to dial up one style over the other because that behavior is needed for a specific set of circumstances and desired outcomes.

# The Solutions-Based Leader

One of the things successful entrepreneurs and corporate executives have in common is their ability to produce results. They are problem solvers, goal oriented, and bottom-line driven. Give them a difficult situation, and within a matter of minutes they will offer a solution. These are the solutions-based leaders.

They are competitive and driven. Once they focus on a target, they just keep moving forward until they reach victory. They keep their eyes on the ball.

Yet as good as that sounds, they have a problem. And it can be a big one. They believe, consciously or subconsciously, they are the only ones that can solve anything. They've lived their lives counting on their personal productivity and find relying on others difficult. They feel they have the right answers—an understanding of exactly what path to follow when achieving goals. They rule others by giving directions, doling out orders, and preferring to be in control.

As a sole proprietor or a new supervisor, solutions-based leadership is a must. It is a necessary practice and the first step to achievement. The problem appears when the entrepreneur starts hiring employees and the supervisor moves up the ladder.

Throughout this growing period, solutions-based leaders need to utilize other leadership traits in order to sustain success. They must learn the only way they can continue on their path to victory is now through the accomplishments of others. It is a change from having all the answers to letting others find the way. It is done through trust, delegation, and letting go.

## Traits of the Solutions-Based Leader

1. Driven: Possesses a strong sense of obligation to get things done; propelled or motived by something

2. Goal-oriented: Works hard to achieve results; places great value on achieving desired outcomes

3. Competitive: Enjoys winning; has a strong desire to be the best

4. Focused: Concentrates on the end result; motivated by reaching specific objectives

5. Solution centered: Looks for resolution first; refrains from thinking through the process for reaching a goal

6. Short attention span: Moves on quickly after accomplishments; easily dismisses others' feelings when giving direction

# The Servant-Centered Leader

These individuals focus on being of service to others; they are interested in people and like to please, gaining great satisfaction from building relationships. They enjoy working in a team-based environment.

The benefit to this leadership style is their understanding of how to get things done through others. They are instinctively in tune with how people think and feel. Servant-centered leaders not only comprehend the needs of their employees, but they have an excellent handle on customer requirements as well. This leader draws a big following, is dedicated to aiding others, and is well liked.

Yet for all their good intentions, servant-centered leaders have their challenges. Too often they let their desire to please get in the way of making tough calls. They find difficulty making sound business decisions that may encompass cutting back on benefits, shrinking expenses, and even downsizing.

Entrepreneurs that fit this leadership style may have suffered during a downturned economy because of their struggle between declining sales and tightening spending. They often hold off on making hard-hitting choices until it is too late. The internal struggle servant-centered leaders face can sometimes be paralyzing.

The traits of the servant-centered leader are absolutely necessary in a quest for greatness. Yet, as with anything, excessive behavior—even when it is centered on serving others—can also be damaging.

## Traits of the Servant-Centered Leader

1. Non-judgmental: Values individuality; respects the views and opinion of others

2. Collaborative: Works well with others; strives for win-win outcomes

3. Team-oriented: Stresses the importance of teamwork; concentrates on a synergistic approach to reaching goals

4. Empathetic: Understands the feelings, thoughts and attitudes of others; very caring

5. Hesitant: Struggles with making difficult decisions that negatively impact people; can become uncertain, tentative, and slow in taking action

6. Apprehensive: Becomes paralyzed when making tough decisions; very uneasy with taking things away from people, i.e. layoffs, benefits, reduced hours, etc.

# The Process-Driven Leader
・・・・・・・・・・・・

Process-driven leaders are focused on method. They are thinkers and enjoy analyzing. They prefer systematically moving from one step to another and are very orderly and sensible. Their energy is spent in thinking about things versus physical activity. They minimize conversations and are much more relaxed expressing themselves in writing. Texting, e-mails, and the written word are their favored methods of communication.

This leader prefers facts over feelings, working well with rules and regulations. They operate efficiently, setting measurements for goals that will then coincide with established timelines. Process-driven leaders do not miss deadlines and are extremely accountable for their personal outcomes. They draw conclusions based on reason and concrete facts, needing time to prepare and plan.

It is this logical, rational approach, however, that can also serve as their demise.

Because process-driven leaders need to work in a controlled environment, they lack the ability to make quick decisions, take risks, and be spontaneous. Due to their linear thinking, they find difficulty visualizing the abstract. Those around them believe they can be unrealistic and hardheaded. They appear difficult to get to know, are not viewed as being people persons, and struggle when collaborating with others.

Their matter-of-fact approach does not appear endearing; Instead, their well-thought-out plans are viewed as restricted thinking and their structured procedures are considered inflexible. They can appear aloof, uncaring, and standoffish. The real problem for the process-driven leader is the difficulty they face when they are trying to change. Because they do not readily display their emotions, they can appear resistant to change even when they are on board with new ideas.

## Traits of the Process-Driven Leader

1. Methodical: Uses processes for getting things done; focuses on the how

2. Systematic: Thinks step-by-step; acts according to a fixed plan or system

3. Organized: Uses structure to coordinate or carry out activities; has rules for doing or planning things

4. Rational: Makes decisions based on facts or reason and not on emotions or feelings; exercises reason, sound judgment, and good sense

5. Perfectionist: Refuses to accept any standard short of perfection; becomes displeased with anything that does not meet extremely high standards
6. Inflexible: Becomes unwilling to change when the process is challenged; difficulty thinking outside the box

# The Financially-Focused Leader

Financially-focused leaders revel in the numbers. They have strong math skills, can do most calculations in their head, and drive results according to financial outcomes. They use functions like analysis, forecasting, and interpretation to make decisions and incorporate financial control into their management effectiveness.

They interpret data to get their perspective of a financial situation and use this viewpoint to set direction. They are goal oriented and measure results in terms of numbers, statistics, and percentages. Financially-focused leaders routinely run various reports to validate their findings, comparing actual performance with planned objectives.

They are extremely accurate, pay close attention to details, and approach their work systematically. Their organizational skills combined with their keen ability to analyze, evaluate, and study are invaluable. Yet again this leadership style is another testament to strengths becoming a detriment when it comes to the creative and people side of the business. The financially-focused leader's emphasis on measurements, indicators, and calculations are the very opposite of the imaginative. Their preference to deal with data is contradictory to building relationships. This disconnect causes chaos, which is unpredictable and foreign to this leader.

## Traits of the Financially-Focused Leader

1. Mathematical: understands and calculates the impact of actions on ideas and objects and the relationship between them; good with numbers, formulas, and calculations

2. Economical: Gives good value or service in relation to the amount of money, time, or effort spent; avoids extravagance

3. Analytical: Follows trends to make projections; utilizes forecasting to make decisions; focuses on gross profit, return on investment to make decisions; understands revenue/expense impact

4. Frugal: Saves and invests wisely; not wasteful—keeps a close eye on expenses

5. Reluctant: Unwilling to take risks without some guarantee; resists decisions that lack in tangible benefits

6. Analysis paralysis: Over-analyzes or over thinks situations so a decision is delayed or action is never taken; may lead to missed opportunities

# The Visionary Leader

Visionary leaders are possibility thinkers, always considering what-ifs and dismissing limitations. They are innovative and use change as an inspiration to do great things. They like to reinvent and start over. Doing things different just for the sake of it motivates them. They are able to build upon their dreams and ideas, using visualization to create their reality. They look to build a better mousetrap, leading others by revolutionizing the way work gets done, enhancing products, and setting new direction.

Nothing is impossible in the world of a visionary leader. They learn from their competition and seek ways to do things differently. Give them a whiteboard, and they will draw circles, squares, and triangles, connecting them with lines and arrows. With a mind that works like a pinball machine, they are all over the board with their thought process. What begins looking like confusion and disorder results in greater innovation, modernization, and advancement.

For every person that places the visionary leader on a pedestal, another finds them frustrating. They are viewed as emotional, unorthodox, and scatterbrained. They become the enemy with their idealistic approach, pie-in-the-sky concepts, and out-of-the-box thinking. Because they have difficulty moving from one step to the next in a systematical manner, they shut down trying to communicate with their skeptics, who in turn lose faith in their leadership.

## Traits of the Visionary Leader

1. Innovative: Enjoys change; focuses on introducing new ideas, devices, and methods

2. Unrestrictive: Imagines the possibilities; views people and situations without limitations or boundaries

3. Pioneering: Opens up new areas of thought, research, and development; considers problems as opportunities

4. Futuristic: Easily expresses visions of the future; ahead of the times and revolutionary in their thinking

5. Idealistic: Represents things in their ideal forms, rather than as they are; overlooks the details to turn their dreams into reality

6. Indecisive: Experiences difficulty with implementation; often hard to follow and understand

# The Charismatic Leader

You know charismatic leaders when they walk into a room. They have a certain magnetism that draws people to them. They always seem to know what to say, how to engage even the shyest individual, and just make people feel good. Their optimistic approach keeps them energized and full of life. They laugh easily and rarely face adversity.

They are very convincing, using their selling skills to motivate, close deals, and win people over. Charismatic leaders have a way about them that can lift up even the saddest individual. Their ability to make people feel special is hypnotizing. They are often powerful speakers; when they talk, people listen. They captivate their audience.

These are the charming individuals that can strike up a conversation with anyone, and they actually care about what the other person has to say. Charismatic leaders stay engaged in their conversations and listen with the intent to understand versus to respond. They listen with their eyes by staying present in their interactions with others. Their attention is turned away from outside influences with a concentration on the other person.

The challenge this leader faces is often the result of

jealousy. They can appear to have it all and be viewed as insincere and conceited. Their charm can look like a cover-up for a lack of intelligence. The presence that works in their favor when drawing people toward them can become their enemy when used in excess. The charismatic leader then turns into being unconvincing, unbearable, and someone people want to run from.

## Traits of the Charismatic Leader

1. Influential: Uses persuasive skills to gain consensus; possesses the capacity to have an effect on the character, development, or behavior of another

2. Believable: Relies on credibility to build a reputation of speaking the truth; retains a convincing style when communicating

3. Approachable: Maintains a friendly, agreeable, and welcoming attitude; easy to talk to

4. Optimistic: Looks on the more favorable side of things; expects the most promising outcome

5. Unrealistic: Relies on personal charm to a detriment; utilizes emotional manipulation rather than reason

6. Egotistical: Dominates the opinion of others; becomes absorbed in oneself and is self-centered

## In Closing

As you read through each of the six styles of leadership, you likely identified more with one or two than with the others. Yet, you have bits and pieces of them all. The key to kaleidoscope leading is to know when you need to rely on each one in order to further your goals and objectives.

# II
*The Six Beliefs of a
Kaleidoscope Leader*

Now that you have an understanding for the six styles of leadership that make up the components of the kaleidoscope leader, the next step is to explore what this leader believes in. The kaleidoscope leader's philosophy is that an individual's success is predicated on the success of others. In carrying out this manner of leading, here are the six beliefs they practice:

1. Put Others First
2. Take Ownership
3. Foster an Optimistic Attitude
4. Drive Results Through the Details
5. Inspire Others
6. Practice Lifelong Learning

These six beliefs are dedicated to the success of others. Each one is based on the trust that the more successful others are, the more success the kaleidoscope leader experiences. By combining these beliefs, one reaches greater personal achievement. It is an understanding that everyone is interdependent on one another, and through these synergistic relationships greatness is experienced due to this interconnectivity.

As you read through this next section, you will explore how these styles and beliefs all blend together, simulating the turning of a kaleidoscope to form different images. Each image is perfect within itself, yet reliant on one another, creating the many facets of leadership.

Likewise, each one of the six beliefs relies heavily on the other five. They comingle, reinforcing the overall belief of the kaleidoscope leader's philosophy. For example, maintaining an optimistic attitude inspires others. Individuals that put others first are committed, accountable, and highly responsive. People that practice lifelong learning pay attention to the details. The combination of the six leadership styles (solutions-based, servant-centered, process-driven, charismatic, financially focused, and visionary) are equally synergistic. The blend of the six styles with the six beliefs creates the multifaceted kaleidoscope leader.

# Put Others First

*Be interested instead of interesting.*

## Stay Present and in the Moment

Staying present and in the moment is to remove distractions and to focus on the now. It is to be completely aware of the moment at hand. This is sometimes one of the most difficult leadership behaviors to realize because it is contrary to what is traditionally taught about leading. Instead of staying in the moment, we are encouraged to multitask. The individual that can balance the most plates, as in a circus act, is the most admired. Yet when you put others first, you realize that your attention must stay in the present.

Staying in the moment means closing your laptop, turning off your cell phone, and concentrating on the conversation at hand. It is listening with your eyes when you are talking with someone. It means opening an awareness of everything that is going on at that very instant, suspending thoughts about your the next meeting, project, or task on your to-do list. It is keying in on the current interaction and releasing thoughts of the past or future. By staying present and in the moment, your full attention is drawn to the now, and you are letting go of all interferences.

## Refrain from Judgment

Passing judgment is a developed skill. When we were small children we probably played with everyone and anyone. It didn't matter what the color of their skin was or how they sounded. It probably didn't even matter what toys they preferred. As we grew older we began to filter what was right and wrong, making decisions of who we approved of by the way others looked, the clothes they wore, or the cars they drove. We moved through time, building a method by which we used judgment to guide what was correct and what was not. Eventually, we began making decisions about people that had absolutely no bearing on the truth.

When we put others first, we open our eyes to the facts, to what is real and genuine about others. We may not agree with a particular lifestyle or political view of someone, but we refrain from judgment. Just because it is not in alignment with our own beliefs doesn't mean it is wrong. In fact, it is just the opposite. It is right in their eyes. We don't have to accept their beliefs. We don't have to walk their path with them. But we must not judge them because their beliefs are different from ours. We must instead embrace their individuality, recognize the differences, and live in acceptance that there are many ways to live a life—ours being just one of them.

## Perform Random Acts of Kindness

Kaleidoscope leaders are naturally kind to others. They treat all individuals with respect and compassion. Therefore, it is only natural that they look for opportunities to be kind when it is not expected. This kindness runs the full gamut, from offering career advice and making introductions to the simple courtesy of opening the door for someone. They can be found in returning a dropped twenty-dollar bill to a congratulatory gift of recognition. It can be as little as a text sent merely because they are thinking of someone to a surprise night of celebration. The size of the gesture and the cost of the item are not important. It is simply the thought, the surprise, and the spontaneity of the moment that makes it special.

And the recipient changes along with the deed. A surprised moment of kindheartedness may be spent on a child, loved one, family member, or a stranger. Kindness can be offered to a long-lost friend, colleague from another department, or neighbor that just moved in next door.

The endeavor and the beneficiary are varied and limitless, yet intentional. The kaleidoscope leader looks for opportunities to offer kindness. A nod of encouragement, a smile, or a simple sign of affection can be as meaningful as a monetary gift. It is the combination of their desire for personal generosity and their realization of the important effect these random acts have over others that keeps the kaleidoscope leader repeating them over and over again.

## Be Interested As Well As Interesting

When practicing kaleidoscope leadership, there is always a need to be paying attention to the other person. The focus must move from within to without, realizing the value of staying present, avoiding distractions, and putting others first. They stay engaged with the other person, listening to their goals and dreams. They move into their world versus pulling them into theirs. They find themselves being interested, not interesting.

Kaleidoscope leaders ask lots of questions. They intently listen to the answers, allowing the responses to drive the direction of the conversation. They listen with the intent to understand before being understood.

This approach encompasses the very idea of putting others first. There is a realization as a leader that nothing can be accomplished without others. It has to all be based on their success being predicated on the success of those around them. By focusing attention on others, they produce meaningful relationships that easily create greatness.

## Enjoy Meeting People That Are Different

One of the most beautiful things we have on earth is the fact that nothing is the same. Snowflakes, fingerprints, zebra stripes, and DNA cannot be duplicated. With atoms always moving energy around, nothing remains unchanged. Change is constant, and different is normal. Think about how boring our world would be if there were no differences, if flowers looked and smelled the same, if all dog lovers had only one puppy to choose from, and if there was only one type of fruit to eat or vegetable to cook. But this isn't our world. Instead we have many pets to love, fruits to grow, and vegetables to eat. And we have many people different from us to enjoy.

Kaleidoscope leaders understand the uniqueness of the universe and how we all connect even when we feel disconnected. They realize the advantage of surrounding themselves with like-minded and unlike-minded individuals. They welcome thoughts different from their own, appreciate another point of view, and respect people that disagree with them. They relish in the differences, considering an alternative way of thinking as exciting. They are curious as to how someone processes information different than their method. They are genuinely interested in learning new customs and traditions. They are not threatened by diverse thinking. They are respectful of those who dress, speak, and act in ways that are dissimilar to themselves.

As they move through the process of seeking out all types of people, they maintain a clear understanding of their core beliefs. They will consider alternative views and may even adapt one or two. But they have the strength and willpower to stay firm when their beliefs cannot be altered. This is when they will agree to disagree. They will accept and respect those who are different, yet realize the importance of staying true to themselves.

## Speak As If the Person Is in the Room

Think about it. Are there times when you say something about someone that you would not say if they could hear you? Have you found yourself making disparaging remarks about another individual that would embarrass you if they ever found out? The answer to both questions is most likely yes. We have all been in situations where we make a comment about a person that we would never want filmed or broadcasted. As much as we know it is wrong to do, we ignore our heart and give in to the temptation. As humans, this temptation is difficult to resist. So begin by filtering your words in your mind before they move to your mouth. Before the words are spoken, ask yourself if you would repeat what you are about to say if that person was in the room with you. Then trust your judgment, which will most likely lead to you refraining from commenting or, at best, revising what you were about to say.

Kaleidoscope leaders realize that in order to try to put others first they must be respectful of who they are and how they feel. This consideration deepens when one considers what they say about someone in their absence. It also speaks volumes for those in the room at the time. The signal kaleidoscope leaders send by not speaking unfavorably about someone absent shows those in the room they will be treated with the same respect.

## Tying the Leadership Style to the Kaleidoscope Belief

Now that you have read through Put Others First, let's examine how this belief affects each of the six styles of leadership.

## *The Solutions-Based Leader's Relationship to Put Others First*

### Tendencies:

- Does not easily accept this belief due to their focus on getting things done and problem solving

- May struggle with the notion of people first due to desire to achieve goals and objectives

### Recommendations:

- Be mindful that goals cannot be accomplished without the involvement of others when driving results

- Pull away from always solving problems on your own and utilize the talent around you for new ideas and approaches

- Divert attention from the goal to the people involved

- Practice acknowledging others for a job well done

## *The Servant-Centered Leader's Relationship to Put Others First*

### Tendencies:

- Easily adapts to this belief
- Prefers to highlight others; recognizes accomplishments other than their own

### Recommendations:

- Individualize methods of recognition to make it more personal
- Consider making tough decisions regarding people sooner versus later
- Be cautious of counting on the opinion of others over your own
- Understand your value as a leader and the necessity to move forward with decisions even when you don't have total buy-in

## *The Process-Driven Leader's Relationship to Put Others First*

### Tendencies:

- Is challenged when focusing on people over procedures

- Prefers to rely on data when making decision versus opinions of others

**Recommendations:**

- Consider all processes are only as good as the people following them
- Utilize the mistakes of others as learning opportunities for them
- Include the advice and suggestions of others when designing processes
- Use your intuition more

## *The Financially-Focused Leader's Relationship to Put Others First*

**Tendencies:**

- Trusts the sure thing over speculation therefore will have difficulty embracing this belief
- Relies heavily on data, information and evidence versus faith in others when making decisions

**Recommendations:**

- Be open minded to the advice of individuals not analytically driven

- Work on building relationships versus working in isolation
- Move from an all-business approach to a more personalized demeanor
- Find opportunities to practice spontaneity

## *The Visionary Leader's Relationship to Put Others First*

### Tendencies:

- Will adapt easily to this belief when in alignment with personal goals
- Is open to recognizing the contributions of others

### Recommendations:

- Maximize the thoughts of others to achieve goals
- Seriously consider ideas foreign to yours
- Be mindful of when it is advantageous to dream and when you need to stay in the moment
- Listen more, allowing others to take the lead when brainstorming or facilitating discussions

## *The Charismatic Leader's Relationship to Put Others First*

### Tendencies:

- Accepts and practices this belief effortlessly
- Comfortable meeting new people and sincerely respects the views of others when aligned with theirs

### Recommendations:

- Look for the value of ideas that are in opposition to your own
- Give up the spotlight, opening up time for others to shine
- Be cautious of playing favorites to those who admire you
- Refrain from dominating situations and relationships

# Take Ownership

*Point the finger in, not out.*

## Hold Yourself Accountable

Kaleidoscope leaders are highly responsive and accountable and take ownership for all they do. They own the expression "Point the finger in, not out." They have a clear understanding of what they are responsible for and accept it without question. This type of leader speaks the truth but doesn't place blame. They build a reputation of being someone that can always be counted on; they are very dependable individuals. They willingly own all that is within their control.

Their actions define ownership. They are always on time, do not miss deadlines, and are true to their word. They do not overcommit. Instead, they exceed expectations. They are reliable. People count on them. They do what they say they will do, consistently perform, and live a life of accountability.

Kaleidoscope leaders have a high level of integrity, don't break promises, and are true to their word.

As simple as this sounds, one of the places a leader gets into trouble is not by lying but by overcommitting. Too often our great intentions cause us to agree to impossible deadlines. When we are trying to be all things to all people, we can easily fall into a trap of overpromising and under-delivering.

The answer is to first be true to yourself. Address commitments honestly. Know your limitations. Hold yourself accountable.

## Delegate to Make Others Great

One of most difficult tasks a new manager faces is delegating. Some individuals look at it as dumping work onto someone else. This feeling is usually partnered with guilt. They sense that they can't ask their staff to do more when they are already overworked. Other managers feel delegation takes too long. Why waste time showing someone how to do something that they can do themselves ten times faster? Another challenge with delegation centers around best practices. Some leaders believe that their way is the right way—the only way. So delegating will only result in inadequacies, rework, and failures.

The truth about delegating is that it makes people great. To not delegate is to prohibit the growth and success of others. To hold on to job duties, projects, and assignments can be a selfish act that stops others from developing.

Delegating is simply a method of training and developing employees. It is teaching your staff new skills. Kaleidoscope leaders realize that when their success is predicated on the success of others, assigning work is a manner in which one learns. It is the essence of teaching new skills, expecting satisfactory outcomes, and demonstrating faith in another.

## Believe That You Are What You Tolerate

Take a moment and really think about this statement: You are what you tolerate. As you reflect on it, consider those things in your life that you put up with, attitudes you accept, behaviors you disagree with yet you allow to take place, and conversations that you listen to without stopping or walking away.

What about the excellence you have decided to only tolerate in your life? It may be fine dining, designer clothes, luxurious vacations, or a beautifully furnished home. The things you accept and reject in your life are the essence of who you are.

It holds true with relationships as well as material things. Your level of tolerance can be seen by examining the people and things you have surrounded yourself with over the years. Are your friends or family members disrespectful to you or hold you in high regard? Is your car always cluttered and your clothes in disarray? Or do you take pride in your appearance, the environment you call home, and your personal integrity?

The answers to these questions transcend into your professional life as a leader. Do you allow coworkers to take advantage of you? Do you accept poor performance from an employee because it is easier than addressing it? A kaleidoscope leader only tolerates the best—in behaviors and surroundings. They expect top performance from their team and good working conditions. They lift their expectations to a high level and will not tolerate anything less.

## Realize You Are a Role Model

The first principle in my book *The Pied Piper Principle: Lead, and They Will Follow* is somebody's always watching. It is based on the premise that people watch everything a leader does—good and bad. And a kaleidoscope leader is no different. Every move they make and every comment they say is being scrutinized. They know this, live with it, and actually use it to their advantage. They realize the impact they make on others and focus their efforts on achieving positive results, inspiring great things, and living a life dedicated to the success of others.

They accept the responsibility for being someone

that others emulate. They realize the impression they leave and understand the power it can have over others. Yet they never take advantage of this status. Instead their emphasis is on doing the right thing at the right time. Kaleidoscope leaders position themselves to help others accomplish goals and achieve results. They do this by modeling the behaviors required to attain greatness.

They do what they say they will do and refrain from gossip and hearsay. They carry themselves in a manner that reflects their greatness. They know they are being watched and are comfortable with the responsibility of being role models. They completely hold themselves accountable in all they do.

## Plan for Interruptions

Kaleidoscope leaders understand the importance of planning. They know the value of time management and keeping to a schedule. Yet they are well aware that things will get off track; even the most thoughtful to-do list can unravel. Therefore, when holding themselves accountable, they plan for interruptions.

This is often one of the obstacles that leaders overlook. As much as we may want to have a day planned down to the minute, life has a way of changing our direction. The unforeseen happens, the least expected situation occurs, and too often a leader feels frustrated and out of control.

Yet if one plans for the unseen occurrences, the leader can continue to hold themselves accountable because they plan for interruptions.

Holding back-to-back meetings seems futile. Common sense tells us that some will run over and others may begin late, disrupting our day. Managers that are caught off guard when an employee calls in sick, a shipment is wrong, or a meeting is suddenly called simply have not planned for interruptions. As we view life and know that it comes with constant change, we must welcome the same alterations in our day-to-day life.

As you prepare your schedule for tomorrow, give yourself some open time. Do this throughout the week and the month. This will allow you flexibility to deal with interruptions. You will find the open moments will quickly fill up but not at the expense of dropping something else. Instead, you will find accountability getting easier and easier by planning for interruptions.

## Rely on a Circle of Influence, Circle of Concern

One of the best business books of all time is *Seven Habits for Highly Effective People* by Stephen Covey. In the first habit (Be Proactive), he introduces the concept of circle of influence, circle of concern. And to this day, it is a theory to live by. If it is the first time you have heard of it, it very well may change your approach on how you view life.

Imagine two circles next to each other on a page. They are exactly the same size. Now picture one labeled *Influence* and the other labeled *Concern*. As you examine them, think about different situations you face in your life and how you approach them. Do you find yourself easily frustrated with things that you can't control? For example, how annoyed do you get when you are caught in a traffic jam? Do you find yourself pounding the steering wheel, weaving in and out of lanes in an attempt to advance your position? Or do you sit back, relax, and turn on your favorite CD?

How about the weather? Will a torrential downpour on your only day off throw you for a loop? Does the cancellation of work due to a record snowstorm cause you anxiety due to lost revenue, or do you find the quietness of snow falling welcoming, offering a reason to curl up with a good book?

Your outlook to situations that are beyond your control define the two circles: *Influence* and *Concern*. If you become annoyed with circumstances you have no bearing on, the circle of Concern grows bigger and bigger while the circle of Influence becomes smaller. Allowing your emotions to be tied directly to things you cannot influence minimizes your power, giving in to a feeling of helplessness, frustration, and anger. And the more you allow it, the bigger the Concern circle gets and the smaller the Influence circle becomes.

However, if you focus your attention on only that which you can influence, the Influence circle grows while the circle of Concern diminishes. In doing this, you place your personal power on things that are within you capacity to impact. You do not let circumstances beyond your control affect you. Instead, the kaleidoscope leader that takes ownership over their feelings directs their attention to the outcomes they can influence.

## Tying the Leadership Style to the Kaleidoscope Belief

Now that you have read through Take Ownership, let's examine how this belief affects each of the six styles of leadership.

### *The Solutions-Based Leader's Relationship to Take Ownership*

#### Tendencies:

- Embraces holding themselves accountable and focuses on what they can influence
- Easily delegates tasks and assignments

### Recommendations:

- Give others the opportunity to solve problems
- Be receptive to ideas, methods, and solutions different than your own
- Assign tasks evenly; avoid always seeking out your "go to" person
- Use the mistakes of others as learning opportunities, and refrain from being overly punitive

## *The Servant-Centered Leader's Relationship to Take Ownership*

### Tendencies:

- Utilizes personal style as an example for others to follow
- Recognizes the contributions of others when delegating

### Recommendations:

- Reevaluate levels of tolerance as you may be too lenient with poor performers
- Remove personal guilt when delegating to those with heavy workloads

- Distribute assignments wisely when deadlines are pressing and you need time to meet them
- Understand and accept that some people will not change no matter how much you try to help them

## *The Process-Driven Leader's Relationship to Take Ownership*

### Tendencies:

- Understands their responsibility of holding themselves accountable for how goals are achieved
- Naturally organizes time for maximum productivity

### Recommendations:

- Gain a better understanding of your personal impact as a role model
- Use the mistakes of others as learning tools, thus opening up your level of tolerance
- Be more accepting of interruptions caused by people versus process deviations
- Assign tasks more often versus doing work yourself

## *The Financially-Focused Leader's Relationship to Take Ownership*

### Tendencies:

- Easily holds others accountable for data, reports, timely information, etc.
- Operates in a factual world with minimal tolerance for ambiguity

### Recommendations:

- Delegate intricate tasks more often
- Be more accepting and open to circumstances that are not financially based and more people focused
- Gain a greater understanding that role modeling takes on many facets
- Utilize mistakes as learning opportunities

## *The Visionary Leader's Relationship to Take Ownership*

### Tendencies:

- Believes strongly in their ability to set direction

- Focuses on what they can influence and removes barriers easily

**Recommendations:**

- Be receptive to the ideas of others versus discounting views opposite of your own
- Utilize your creative nature to encourage others to think innovatively
- Accept your limitations and employ those who bring balance to your pioneering style
- Avoid indecisiveness when assigning work

## *The Charismatic Leader's Relationship to Take Ownership*

**Tendencies:**

- Maintains an inclusive manner when delegating
- Easily gets buy-in when holding others accountable

**Recommendations:**

- Share the spotlight as a role model and lessen your need to be the center of attention
- Avoid over-committing to maintain personal accountability

## Take Ownership

- Be aware of using your persuasive style as a means of manipulation when trying to influence an outcome
- Refrain from delegating menial tasks and saving high profile jobs for yourself

# Foster an Optimistic Attitude

*The optimist sees the glass as half full. The kaleidoscope leader sees the glass as half full and focuses on filling it up all the way.*

## Find Ways to Say Yes

When asked, "Who would you rather follow, a person that leans toward optimism or a pessimist?" the answer will repeatedly be the optimist. It is only natural to want to be around someone that finds the rainbow at the end of the storm. Individuals with an optimistic attitude look for the best possible outcome in all situations—an important trait in the kaleidoscope leader.

As they examine difficult situations and are often faced with following guidelines that may be perceived as constrained and tight, kaleidoscope leaders look for opportunities to say yes. They rephrase a response of "No," into something like: "I'm unable to do that, but what I can do is…" This simple method of looking for a win for everyone can close deals thought forever lost, overcome barriers that stop progress, yet serve to follow rules and guidelines.

If a kaleidoscope leader is faced with negotiating price, instead of telling the prospect they can't come down in cost, they will first determine how much is available to spend and then sell accordingly. Using the statement "I can't offer it at that amount, but what I can do for that price is…" turns a possible negative outcome into a positive one. Discussing time off with an employee can go from "You can't have all of those days off," to "I can't give you all of that time off right now, but what I can do is…" Again, a tweak at how something is worded can move what could have been perceived as a negative outcome to an acceptable alternative. It's all about finding ways to say yes.

## Be a Possibility Thinker

As kaleidoscope leaders consider ways to say yes, they move toward being possibility thinkers. These individuals look at situations with a what-if approach. Doors are not easily closed to opportunity thinkers. They examine all options, seeking for outcomes often hidden in doubt and misfortune.

The possibility thinker fosters optimism with an understanding that when one door closes, another opens. They do not see limitations as negative forces. They look for ways to overcome restrictions. Instead of considering borders to be confining, the kaleidoscope leader looks to expand them. They think out of the box, are innovative, and use visioning as a method from which to build and expand their thought process.

They are natural problem solvers and view difficulties as opportunities. They can quickly access what went wrong and offer solutions. They are willing to be told no and will listen to how something can't be done only to find ways to turn the situation around to a favorable conclusion. This characteristic aligns itself with finding ways to say yes.

They are catalysts for variation, recognizing the need for it, and can remove barriers to create a synergistic environment. They are willing to positively challenge the status quo and will champion change.

## Be Collaborative

As kaleidoscope leaders foster an optimistic attitude, they do it through collaboration. They have a deep understanding of the need to work with others to accomplish lofty goals. Knowing their success is predicated on the success of others, collaborative thinking is natural and inviting. People want to help them and are drawn to their enthusiastic approach because it is viewed as inclusive.

Although they may spearhead projects, oversee departments, or run companies, they don't do it alone. They don't do it *with* people. Instead they do it *through* people. They are quick to gain buy-in, overcome obstacles, and reach consensus. They are skilled at persuasion, effective in the give-and-take of a relationship, and are excellent listeners.

As they work collaboratively, kaleidoscope leaders cultivate opportunities through diversity. They have great respect for and relate well to people from varied backgrounds. They anticipate, recognize, and meet the needs of others, always looking for ways to increase satisfaction and loyalty. Often viewed as trusted advisors, they understand someone's perspective and gladly become engaged in relationships.

As kaleidoscope leaders foster optimistic attitudes collaboratively, they demonstrate a strong sense in what others need in order to thrive. They easily acknowledge and reward people's strengths, accomplishments, and developments. They have a keen ability to read a group's emotional current, understanding the forces that shape the views and actions of others. They foster open communication and stay receptive to bad news as well as good. Yet, when it is all said and done, they seek positive outcomes through their optimistic attitude.

## Dome Up

Doming up is a concept you may find novel and effective. It begins when you are faced with negative situations that are not within your control. It could be times when you get involved in a conversation with a chronic complainer. It may be a period when you are working on a team filled with anger and disillusion. Or it could be in a private conversation where the other party is on a rant about something and can't seem to stop. There may be other circumstances where a speaker is discussing ideas and concepts that are against your beliefs. Because these moments can be undesirable or destructive, you may prefer to disengage, yet are unable to simply walk away or hang up the phone.

When faced with these adverse viewpoints, dome up. How is this done? Picture a glass dome mantel clock. They can stand anywhere from eight to fifteen inches high and have a glass dome covering the timepiece. Now with that in your mind's eye, replace the timepiece with you standing or sitting with a glass dome around you as a shield. This protective mechanism guards you from negativity. It causes the sounds of anger, protests, and grumbles to be muffled and muted. This invisible armor forbids negativity to enter your personal space.

Because it is glass, you are able to see clearly through

to the outside. Yet it motionlessly protects your acceptance. You are able to maintain your personal power, controlling what you can influence, and still be engaged in the moment. You simply do not succumb to undesirable conversations or situations.

Each and every time you are put in a state that you do not want to be involved in and are unable to disengage, dome up. Picture yourself surrounded by the glass shield guarding you from unwanted behaviors and viewpoints. Do not judge the moment; simply protect yourself from its impact.

## Coach the Difference Between Want, Believe, and Know

One of the most valuable things kaleidoscope leaders can do for their employees is coach the difference between want, believe, and know. These are three states of mind that are the driving force behind realizing one's dreams.

Throughout our lives we encounter things we want. They range from love, happiness, and success to more specific desires such as marriage, a great job, and a six-figure income. One challenge with the wants is they are sometimes aligned with someone else's dreams.

Too often we confuse our wants with what others want for us, or what will make us happy verses what

## Foster an Optimistic Attitude

we believe we should have. For example, we may be expected to find employment that pays well versus taking a job that is more in line with our talents and interests. Or we may feel pressured by our own misguided beliefs into marrying someone based on physical appearance or because they come from a good family instead of settling down with someone that we are more compatible with.

It is the kaleidoscope leader's responsibility as a workplace coach to help identify and guide others to understanding what someone really wants in their careers. Once this is determined, the next step is to dig deep into the employee's belief system. It is important to have a frame of reference from the individual to determine if they believe they can actually accomplish their goals. Too often we embrace a goal while still holding onto a core belief that we don't deserve it or it is too lofty for us. Although we can say the goal out loud, and even write it down, we have no conviction about accomplishing it because our minds—unknowingly—still harbor unbelief. The kaleidoscope leader needs to recognize these obstacles and help to set the employee on the right course.

That course—the course one follows that always delivers—is in the knowing. It is the heartfelt belief that a trait is superior, and that a natural ability is highly evolved. It is the effortless knowledge stored inside that beats all odds. This knowing is expected, deeply rooted, and overcomes all doubt.

When an individual combines their wants with a

strong belief and embraces it with a level of knowing it will happen, it will occur. It cannot fail. It is the kaleidoscope leader's responsibility to coach their employees through this journey.

## Be Thankful

The last behavior within Fostering an Optimistic Attitude is to practice gratitude by being thankful. Kaleidoscope leaders have an enormous appreciation for life. They are grateful for the little and big things they experience. They begin their day with a silent appreciation for a night of rest (even if it is interrupted), a refreshing shower, a cup of coffee, and transportation to their destination. They are thankful for their family, work, employees, customers, colleagues, and vendors. They readily acknowledge a job well done. Praise comes easy to them, thanking others in many ways—whether with a smile, hug, or handshake; it is a visible sign of appreciation. They handwrite notes, send e-mails, and text messages of thanks to others often.

They practice random acts of kindness throughout the day. They hold the door, let someone go ahead in line, and pick up dropped items. Giving comes natural. Sincere gratitude is second nature. It is easy to offer thanks for a problem solved, good service, and a job well done.

Foster an Optimistic Attitude

They celebrate simple meals, such as a peanut butter and jelly sandwich, and thoroughly relish a five-course dinner at a fine restaurant. They appreciate technology that makes their life easier and allows them to stay in touch with loved ones by the touch of their fingers on a keyboard or swiping messages on their phone. They smile easily. Due to their grateful spirit, their optimistic attitude shines through naturally.

## Tying the Leadership Style to the Kaleidoscope Belief

Now that you have read through Foster an Optimistic Attitude, let's examine how this belief affects the six styles of leadership.

### *The Solutions-Based Leader's Relationship to Foster an Optimistic Attitude*

#### Tendencies:

- This driven style views obstacles as challenges and comfortably pushes for results

- Thinks outside of the box for solutions and is not easily swayed

**Recommendations:**

- Be aware that a realistic approach to problems isn't viewed as you being pessimistic

- Look for ways to include others in decision making versus isolation

- Take time to identify what is important to others, removing the attention to yourself

- Focus on appreciating others and avoid being viewed as someone that takes things for granted

## *The Servant-Centered Leader's Relationship to Foster an Optimistic Attitude*

**Tendencies:**

- Very inclusive in decision making and seeks to see what drives others

- Naturally optimistic, grateful, and appreciative of the contributions of others

**Recommendations:**

- Be cautious of your strong positive attitude positioning you as unrealistic

- Understand there are times when you will not be able to please everyone

Foster an Optimistic Attitude

- Focus on aligning the dreams and aspirations of others with organizational goals
- Be mindful that your empathetic style may need to be downplayed when making difficult decisions

## *The Process-Driven Leader's Relationship to Foster an Optimistic Attitude*

### Tendencies:

- Practices possibility thinking in a systematic manner
- Will find ways to say yes, providing it is a rational outcome

### Recommendations:

- Search for the positive outcome and be mindful your realistic approach may appear pessimistic
- Seek out and find value in those with opposing viewpoints
- Take time to find out what drives others and work toward helping them achieve goals
- Practice being grateful for little things you may overlook

## *The Financially-Focused Leader's Relationship to Foster an Optimistic Attitude*

### Tendencies:

- Uses possibility thinking when tied into measurable outcomes
- Becomes collaborative when working toward mutually beneficial goals

### Recommendations:

- Avoid becoming viewed as a pessimist when communicating why an idea won't work
- Build relationships outside of the world of finance to open yourself to new ideas
- Place greater intention on what others want and need to feel successful in the workplace
- Look for ways to show gratitude for the intangible

## *The Visionary Leader's Relationship to Foster an Optimistic Attitude*

### Tendencies:

- Naturally practices possibility thinking and finding ways to say yes
- Shows appreciation and gratitude for innovation that others may overlook

### Recommendations:

- Maintain a bit of caution around thinking too innovatively to please others
- When collaborating with others seek and be open to opposing views
- Find ways to include linear thinkers to offer balance and insight to your way of thinking
- Revert to realistic thinking when you find yourself too creative in your approach

## *The Charismatic Leader's Relationship to Foster an Optimistic Attitude*

### Tendencies:

- An optimist at heart relies on a grateful, positive approach to influence others
- Enjoys collaborating and looking for mutually beneficial outcomes

### Recommendations:

- Be mindful of appearing overly zealous, causing others to view you as impractical
- Avoid talking people into things which may be viewed as manipulative
- Understand realists are not pessimists
- Consider negative views as alternative thinking

# Drive Results Through the Details

*What you think about, you bring about.*

## Utilize Goals to Focus on Outcomes

Having goals is a common practice today in all walks of life. Students are given assignments with due dates, and workers are charged to complete projects within specific deadlines. We have SMART goals that focus on: specific, measurable, action oriented, realistic, and timeline. We have time management experts helping us to manage our daily, weekly, and monthly tasks to achieve success. We even find them in our personal life. Dieting encompasses how much of what food to eat how often. Exercise comes in the form of how long we work out, how many laps we run, and how many times a week. We are a society obsessed with living a life focused on goals.

Yet too many times disappointment sets in when these well-intended goals are not accomplished. Sales targets aren't met, projects miss deadlines, and weight isn't lost. The kaleidoscope leader realizes that, in order to accomplish goals, the attention must begin with the outcome. By beginning with the end in mind, goals become an extension of the outcome—a means to the end—not the main drive.

You must have a clear idea of what exactly you want to accomplish before targeting the goals to get there. Targeting hundreds of prospects may be futile if you are going after the wrong buyer. Certain diets or exercise plans may counter your efforts to reach the physical outcome you desire. In order to reach your destination, you need to know first where you are going.

Place your awareness on what you want to accomplish. Narrow it down until it is crystal clear in your mind what you want to achieve. Tie in the understanding of the difference among what you want, what you believe is possible, and what you know in your heart is true. Then, and only then, should you decide on the process that will drive your goals toward your desired outcomes.

## Realize It Is All About Execution

As much as we just reviewed focusing on your desired outcomes first, the next and equally important step is in execution. High expectations, grand goals, dreams of success can only become a reality through execution—doing something to advance the process,

## Drive Results Through the Details

moving forward, and overcoming obstacles. The kaleidoscope leader understands the necessity of implementation.

Every goal must have a plan that is carried out. It needs owners—individuals who will hold themselves accountable. It requires people who take responsibility for making things happen. In order to become a successful leader, you have two vital tasks to carry out when it comes to execution.

First, you must find the talent to carry out the mission. These are people who understand what it means to own outcomes. They are the individuals who always volunteer for more, have an unlimited amount of energy, and are always ready and available. They point the finger in, versus out, when it comes to problem resolution. They seek ways to get things accomplished versus allowing obstacles to bring them down.

Your second responsibility for execution is to understand that you are responsible for these talented people you have selected. They are your conduit for making things happen. They require you to praise the little and the big wins. They need to hear when they have fallen off track and when it is time to celebrate their victories.

The kaleidoscope leader becomes the conductor of the orchestra, leading each member to play their instrument at the right time with the right sound to execute the desired melody.

## Have an Understanding of the Financial Impact of Decisions

This comes naturally for financially-focused leaders because their natural tendencies lend themselves to the numbers. Yet for many of the other leadership styles, the financial impact of decisions is unclear and often daunting. There are many well-intended small business owners who do not understand their profit-and-loss statement, become negligent with their banking, and often delay in collecting their money.

Kaleidoscope leaders do not have to be accounting majors. They can easily rely on their CFO, CPA, or accountant to maintain their financial records. But they still need to have the basic understanding of the financial impact of their decisions. Just because a business is in a sudden upturn doesn't necessarily mean it is time to expand space or add new employees. And during a downturn, it doesn't mean that cutbacks and layoffs should be delayed in hopes that things will change.

As with cause and effect, each business decision comes with some ramification—sometimes good and sometimes bad. As with establishing goals and utilizing execution to accomplish them, you need to always consider the financial aspect of your decisions. The consequence of paying people too much or too little can have an enormous impact on your business. Negotiating pennies when it comes to buying big can drastically affect your bottom line. Price increases can take you out of the market or move you to greater profitability.

Once you have embraced the realization of your financial decisions, there is one last offer for consideration. Never lose sight of how adding value to all that you do positively affects your success. The little things that don't cost you are often worth the most—smiling first, caring about the people you deal with, complimenting, being highly responsive, apologizing for mistakes, and offering thanks for a job well done.

These practices come natural for a kaleidoscope leader and are priceless.

## Revisit the Process Often

Kaleidoscope leaders never get comfortable with the way things are done. They understand the need to reinvent and make changes. They are constantly seeking methods to improve and enhance. Revisiting the process is important, and they do it often.

Ignoring change, refusing to believe they may have been outthought or outplayed is often the demise of many leaders. This can be avoided by simply examining what is being done and brainstorming how it can be done better. It begins with the concept that everything one does may be improved. This thought process is confident and self-assured in the ability to set and achieve high standards. When viewed as a positive perspective toward a greater gain, it moves from a defeatist attitude to a winning one.

An effective approach to revisiting a process is to consider it as continuous quality improvement. Every day we find technological advancements pushing us to communicate better, faster, and more efficiently. Would this be the case if great minds settled or did not seek new and better ways to connect?

One way of revamping the way you do things is to ask for the input of an outsider. Seek someone you trust and has no vested interest in your outcomes. Often a detached view offers the most significant recommendations. Suggestions from these sources are uninhibited because there is no history, preconceived notions, or "We've always done it this way." The freedom from fixed thinking opens the doors of endless possibilities.

Your role as a kaleidoscope leader is to constantly reinvent, reengineer, and revisit processes over and over again with the zealous intention to improve.

## Understand the Importance of the Little Things

It is always important to consider the big picture. Focused outcomes originate with visionary thinking. Execution then sets the wheels in motion, which turns thoughts into reality. And along the way the kaleidoscope leader understands the importance of the little things. They take into account facts that may not matter to others. They have a reputation for noticing minor details that, when overlooked, may not make an immediate impact but can also become their demise.

These kaleidoscope leaders are early for gatherings, follow agendas, spell-check before hitting send, and confirm appointments. They start and stop their meeting on time, demonstrating respect for the attendees. They have tidy office spaces and cars. They dress appropriately for each occasion. They aren't disheveled, sloppy, or visually disorganized.

The details they attend to are found in all aspects of their work—from making sure the right people are invited to events and meetings to thoughtfully deciding who needs to be included in memos, e-mail, and text communication. They utilize the fine points when recognizing good performance with an understanding that complimenting the smallest actions often offers the biggest payoff.

These leaders typically have pet peeves as to what is important ranging from error-free reports and hitting deadlines to assuring guests are treated in a certain manner. They like welcome boards in the lobby and meals ordered to specifications. The kaleidoscope leader doesn't get bogged down in the minutia as they have a clear understanding what detail is worth paying attention to, which sets them apart from others.

## Don't Make the Same Mistakes Over and Over

Making mistakes is natural. We all do it, and most of us learn from them. Some believe the only way to success is by trial and error. These individuals believe nothing comes without pain and tribulation. Others take a more positive approach, viewing mistakes as learning opportunities but aren't a necessity to accomplishments.

Whichever approach you prefer, practicing kaleidoscope leadership simply states, if you are going to make a mistake, don't repeat it over and over. It is inexcusable to not learn from mishaps, especially after they happen twice. Yet we see it all the time—whether it is going through a fast-food drive-through and leaving with an incorrect order to receiving a shipment missing part of the inventory.

As a kaleidoscope leader you must realize driving results through the details is getting it right the first time, and certainly by the second time. You need to put in a process where once a problem occurs, you stop to examine what steps to take to eliminate it from happening again. Too often we are so busy recovering from the problem, we move on as soon as we feel we have satisfied the current condition. This well-intended approach never looks back as to how it occurred in the first place. By implementing a continuous quality improvement process that instantaneously fixes the error first and then assures there is no repeat performance, you are guaranteed mistakes don't happen over and over.

## Tying the Leadership Style to the Kaleidoscope Belief

Now that you have read through Drive Results Through the Details, let's examine how this belief affects the six styles of leadership.

## *The Solutions-Based Leader's Relationship to Drive Results Through the Details*

### Tendencies:

- Focuses on goals and desired outcomes naturally
- Drives personal performance on achieving results

### Recommendations:

- Avoid missing important factors due to primary focus on objective
- Consider what it will take to implement your ideas and solutions
- Work toward getting it right with minimal rework
- Seek the opinions of others as to what you missed or overlooked

## *The Servant-Centered Leader's Relationship to Drive Results Through the Details*

### Tendencies:

- Places high value on the implication of details that impact others

- Willing to do rework if the benefit drives individual performance

### Recommendations:

- Maintain a healthy balance between the individual and organizational goals
- Take time to review financial impact of decisions and avoid only looking at humanistic outcomes
- Utilize your value of the contributions of others to achieve results
- Maximize your desire to be inclusive to form strong implementation teams

## *The Process-Driven Leader's Relationship to Drive Results Through the Details*

### Tendencies:

- Completely understands the necessity for planned implementation to drive results
- Embraces rational thinking to minimize and eliminate mistakes that cause rework

### Recommendations:

- Avoid analysis paralysis that can delay decisions to move forward
- Keep in mind financial implications when planning flawless execution
- Understand the goal drives the process—not the other way around
- Utilize your ability to consider details others may overlook to make quicker decisions

## *The Financially-Focused Leader's Relationship to Drive Results Through the Details*

### Tendencies:

- Naturally keeps projects in alignment with budgetary goals
- Identifies early possible derailments in achieving results

### Recommendations:

- Be open to changes in processes that do not have a monetary impact

- Understand added value is not always measured in dollars
- Respect and support the decisions of others when it comes to reworking a process
- Avoid isolation due to your heightened desire to control all financial decisions

## *The Visionary Leader's Relationship to Drive Results Through the Details*

### Tendencies:

- Willing to try new approaches when goals aren't met
- Views mistakes as learning opportunities over setbacks

### Recommendations:

- Work on expanding recommendations beyond visionary outcomes
- Consider the financial impact on what it will take to implement goals
- Focus on expanding your ability to think things through
- Minimize errors using realistic ideas

## *The Charismatic Leader's Relationship to Drive Results Through the Details*

### Tendencies:

- Open to minimizing mistakes that will drive favorable outcomes

- Easily relies on others to execute and implement processes

### Recommendations:

- Avoid dismissing the little things in lieu of big picture objectives

- Be willing to spend time reviewing work before giving final approval

- Welcome the views of the others that have higher attention to details

- Utilize your persuasive style to drive others through implementation

# Inspire Others

*You can open doors for people, but they have to be the ones to walk through.*

## Be Passionate

Passion is defined as an intense emotion, compelling feeling, enthusiasm, or desire for something. It can be the driving force for why people want to follow kaleidoscope leaders. It pulls people to them, drawing them in and energizing everyone it touches.

It can be heard in your voice and seen in your actions. People driven by passion seem to have an unlimited amount of energy, feel optimistic about their endeavors, and are contagious to be around. You can catch their passion, which is key to inspiring others.

Think of the individuals you have worked with that come in already tired first thing in the morning. They are late for meetings, delay projects, easily judge others, and have a diminished amount of energy. They are dispassionate about life, and it shows in everything they do.

Then consider the colleague that always seems to be

"up." They are enthusiastic about the little things, finding positive outcomes to difficult situations because they are ardent about life. They embrace the gift of being alive and accept challenges as opportunities versus setbacks.

Passion is a driving force for all kaleidoscope leaders; they don't run out of it. Instead it builds as they use it to inspire others.

## Be Fair, Consistent, and Honest

Inspiring others calls for consistency, fairness, and honesty. Kaleidoscope leaders that practice this are known for their sincerity. Basing their success on the success of others, they realize the necessity of treating everyone with a sense of objectivity.

Employees prefer and welcome honest feedback. They want to be told the truth—being recognized for the good and the bad. They appreciate advice, suggestions, and recommendations that are specific to their performance. A kaleidoscope leader realizes vague comments like "You need to be more customer service focused" or "You must pay more attention to the details" are meaningless without explicit examples of where the employee fell short.

When dealing with unwelcomed behavior, one must cite exactly what was wrong so the employee knows what needs to be corrected. For example, if an employee is disrespectful to a customer, you need to replay back to them the occurrence, using their words, tone, and body language so they understand what they did incorrectly. Then you need to fully explain what you expect. This is not a time for assuming they know what you are looking for. No matter how minor, the clearer you are in describing your expectation, the better. In fact, to make sure you have communicated properly, ask the employee to explain back to you what they heard. This will eliminate any miscommunication on either party's behalf. Giving negative feedback becomes easy when it is offered with the intention to help another reach greater success.

## Understand the Importance of Timing

One definition of timing is "a function of finding the right balance between supply and demand." This makes sense when applying the word to a new product entering the market, but what about the importance of timing when interacting with people? Kaleidoscope leaders are masters at reading the environment, understanding someone's emotions, and utilizing these skills to add timing to their technique of inspiring others.

Timing is saying the right thing at the right time. It is holding off on making a move because circumstances are wrong, people are on edge, and ideas aren't welcome. It is using the ability to size up a situation and make a move accordingly. When mixed with the right intentions, timing can only bring about positive outcomes.

Problems can occur with timing when you don't place the other person's needs before your own. Instead of having patience, you jump into situations too early, hoping for quicker results. This lack of judgment will almost always cost you, and timing can't be reused. Once the moment is rushed, it is very difficult to start again.

One key lesson is to understand that timing is very individualized. You must be tuned in to others' needs. For example, some people are early birds, so good timing for them is early in the morning and bad timing is late in the day. Some people let their stomachs rule; talk to them when they are hungry and you will miss an opportunity. Fatigue will cost you, as will highly emotional moments.

In order to use time to your advantage, realize it is all about the other guy. Conversations, questions, and recommendations must come when it is in the best interest of the other person, not when it is good for you. This is most important aspect of utilizing timing.

## Have Presence

Presence is often hard to describe, yet when you meet someone that has it, you know it instantly. It has nothing to do with weight, height, or age. It is not reserved for the handsome or beautiful. It does not correspond with position in life, one's title, or professional status. Yet it is visible. It is an air of confidence, grace, and a knowing of one's capacity.

Kaleidoscope leaders that have presence are typically comfortable in all settings. They have the unique capacity to adjust easily to their surroundings and can tune in to the feelings of others, adjusting their style to maximize most situations. This presence magnetically draws people to them. They are easy to be around, at ease in a crowd or in one-on-one meetings.

The question is, how do I acquire presence? It begins with a complete understanding of your strengths and weaknesses. You must build upon your positive attributes and call upon them whenever possible. Capitalize on your strong points to a position of power. Yet be careful to not be viewed as egotistical. Be cautious of the tipping point that moves from humility to arrogance.

Keep in mind, having presence is not reserved for the extrovert. The modest, reserved individual can possess it as well. These are the individuals that remain silent in meetings until the right moment. At the precise time when they speak, the room becomes quiet, everyone pausing to hear what is being said. Their presence is observed very differently than the more outgoing individual, yet is as powerful.

Picture yourself at your best, confident in your abilities, appreciative of your strengths—the very best you.

Watch your body language as you move through this visualization. You may be sitting up straighter, your head may be lifted, or you may be smiling inside and out. This is the presence possessed by the kaleidoscope leader.

## Get the Vote of Others

What if the next time you were up for a promotion the decision was made by consensus? Instead of receiving the advancement due to merit, you had to be voted in to the position—just like the politician. Do you think you would win enough votes to be promoted? Being voted in to a promotion can certainly give you some interesting food for thought. Consider this unusual notion as a means to identifying how collaborative you are, how you are viewed by others as being approachable and believable.

At this very moment there are members of your personal fan club. They are those who believe in you and automatically support you. They have an emotional bank account with you, making deposits of trust and occasionally taking a withdrawal when entering disagreements or change in views. This emotionally charged account has enough deposits that it would be difficult to drain. The people in which you share this tight bond would automatically vote you in for your promotion. These are those who will automatically vote for you

The next group is neutral. They have no strong feelings either way. You haven't offended them, turned them against you, nor positioned them as supporters in your efforts. With them you can just as easily win or lose their vote for advancement.

The last assembly of individuals is definitely not in your camp. Somewhere along the line you have either rubbed them the wrong way or, even worse, they heard something about you and have formed an opinion based on nothing but hearsay. Not only will they not give you their vote, they may even work against you to influence the decision of others.

The message here is understanding your role as a kaleidoscope leader encompasses forming, nurturing, and growing relationships at all levels with all people. You need to pursue a collaborative style of communication to assure those voting for you will do so unequivocally, invest in relationships with the neutral voter to gain their confidence and respect, and identify how you can turn your naysayers into fans.

## Give Credit

When kaleidoscope leaders put others first, they repeatedly practice giving credit to others. They are willing to share a wealth of recognition by allowing those around them to celebrate success. They look for opportunities to give praise and positive reinforcement. And often they offer this encouragement one person at a time.

There are employee engagement surveys that measure how frequently employees are recognized every seven days for a job well done. The outcome suggests that the more often workers are praised while on the job, the more they will produce, stay loyal, and enjoy their employment. Very often this simple task of offering recognition gets lost in good intentions. Managers dealing with challenges and faced with adversity often lose sight of the need to give positive acknowledgements. Instead they focus on negative outcomes that demotivate and demoralize.

Of course, poor performance needs to be addressed. It should come shortly after the offense occurs and should be done in private. Specific expectations with consequences for repeat offenders should be communicated clearly. The kaleidoscope leader understands the importance of addressing negative behavior, the timing involved, and setting the expectations for moving forward.

Yet this same leader never loses sight of the positive contributions employees will give when recognized for the good they do.

## Tying the Leadership Style to the Kaleidoscope Belief

Now that you have read through Inspire Others, let's examine how this belief affects the six styles of leadership.

### *The Solutions-Based Leader's Relationship to Inspire Others*

#### Tendencies:

- Uses their individual drive to achieve goals as a means of motivating others
- Demonstrates passion by exceeding high levels of performance

#### Recommendations:

- Understand your short attention span can appear dismissive and demotivating
- Be mindful of acknowledging others for accomplishments you consider the norm
- Recognize the importance of considering all ideas even though you may not agree with them

- When giving honest feedback, be aware of the importance of timing

## *The Servant-Centered Leader's Relationship to Inspire Others*

### Tendencies:

- Easily inspires others while valuing individuality
- Has a unique ability to realize and apply timing toward mutually beneficial outcomes

### Recommendations:

- Refrain from the need to give equal credit to everyone, understanding it is acceptable to offer additional recognition to those who exceed over others
- Draw upon your personal passion to create a stronger presence
- Avoid putting off addressing unwelcomed behavior
- Understand not everyone will give you their vote and don't take it personal

## *The Process-Driven Leader's Relationship to Inspire Others*

### Tendencies:

- Embraces fairness, consistency, and honesty in the workplace
- Understands the impact of timing when dealing with getting things accomplished

## *Recommendations:*

- Conscientiously draw upon your rational approach to ignite passion to inspire
- Open your awareness to the aspect of timing that relates to moods and emotions
- Work toward shifting your methodical manner to one that is receptive to new ideas
- Be generous in sharing praise and recognition for jobs well done

## *The Financially-Focused Leader's Relationship to Inspire Others*

### Tendencies:

- Completely embraces impartiality, reliability, and stability to stimulate positive outcomes

- Readily considers timing when forecasting results, avoiding impetuous decisions that may cause negative outcomes

### Recommendations:

- Open your awareness of the impact of your presence when dealing with others
- Be mindful of the balance between tangible and intangible outcomes
- Take risks in allowing others to see your sensitive side
- Carve out time to spend meeting with people to discuss non-work related topics

## *The Visionary Leader's Relationship to Inspire Others*

### Tendencies:

- Innovative tendencies are appealing which can position you as approachable
- Your possibility thinking manner allows you to individualize how you motivate others

### Recommendations:

- Understand your idealistic thinking may drive analytic thinkers away
- Be aware your willingness to be creative may cause you to appear inconsistent in your decisions
- Remind yourself to give credit for the ideas of others that enhanced your own
- Embrace the concept of timing and learn when to hold back to be more effective

## *The Charismatic Leader's Relationship to Inspire Others*

### Tendencies:

- Being an inspiration to others is a natural tendency of yours and one you rely on often
- Your magnetic style draws people to you and enhances your overall presence

### Recommendations:

- Realize your influential manner may be viewed as insincere when used in excess
- Stay cognizant of the down side of being too op-

timistic as it can be viewed as unrealistic and naïve

- Keep others' needs in mind to utilize timing in their best interest versus a somewhat selfish approach to being the center of attention
- Be aware of sharing credit for ideas and looking for ways to acknowledge others

# Practice Lifelong Learning

*What you pay attention to grows.*

## Stay in Mental Shape

Kaleidoscope leaders understand the necessity of lifelong learning by keeping their brains in shape. They realize the importance of being well-informed of current events, industry trends, best practices, and innovations. They utilize all forms of communication to be in the know. Today's technology eliminates the excuse of not being a reader. Blogs, YouTube, and Twitter make staying informed easy and fast. The Internet offers the answers to any question possible. Tips for everything, from leadership to running a business, managing top performers to the poor ones, can be found in a few keystrokes.

But staying in mental shape isn't just keeping up to date. It is also about self-improvement. The kaleidoscope leader is in a constant mode of learning and exploring, seeking new ways of doing things and different approaches to old ways of operating. The lifelong learner is always on a quest of self-discovery.

They seek out opportunities to exercise their brain by concentrating on what they think about. They are keenly aware of how their thoughts shape their reality. This awareness drives them to consciously pick and choose what they think about. Negative thoughts are quickly identified and either completely removed or redirected toward more positive viewpoints.

Many use meditation as a form of exercise for their mental power. Others take time throughout the day to take a pause. This internal time-out allows kaleidoscope leaders to center their thoughts, assuring they are staying in mental shape.

## Respect and Value the Differences in One Another

As a lifelong learner, kaleidoscope leaders realize the value each person offers as a unique human being. They welcome new thoughts and ideas. They seek out differences of opinions and learn from them. They have a clear understanding that they do not need to conform to foreign ideas. Instead, they value insights opposite to their own.

And just as kaleidoscope leaders encourage a different approach or another way of looking at something, they bring "agreeing to disagree" into the forefront. They seek innovative thinkers that offer solutions they hadn't thought of. They work to uncover concepts and philosophies unexplored or even considered radical and impossible.

With an open mind they seek first to understand and then to be understood. In doing this, they never lose sight of their convictions. They hold dear personal values and beliefs while passing no judgment on new ways of thinking. As the kaleidoscope leader values and respects new ways of living, they find this lifelong learning process one of enlightenment and illumination.

## Understand the Power of Observation

Kaleidoscope leaders utilize the power of observation to learn and grow. They use silence in an effort to quietly absorb their surroundings. They are tuned in to their environment and can easily assess situations based on what they are seeing and hearing. It is this keen awareness that allows them to tap into their intuitive side for answers.

Their internal radar is always on. They listen and watch. They pay attention to the little things. They notice what others miss—unusual behavior, individuals acting differently, unexpected tardiness, missed deadlines, functions that are suddenly out of balance.

They assess the political climate of a meeting, paying attention to who sits where and who speaks when. They pick up quickly the tone of the gathering and adjust accordingly, wisely adapting their style to maximize their effectiveness.

They are watchful of others and use observation to learn how to alter their behavior to enhance their communication style. Combining their natural talents and skills while embracing the cultural overtone of a situation, kaleidoscope leaders use the power of observation to increase their emotional intelligence through self-regulation.

## Practice Emotional Intelligence

Emotional intelligence originates with self-awareness and self-regulation. Self-awareness combines a deep understanding of one's strengths and areas of opportunity for development. EI (emotional intelligence) then moves to self-regulation—maximizing strengths and improving weaknesses. Much has been written and taught on this topic. It is a primary factor in executive coaching whereby the coach works to bring awareness to strengths and weaknesses then encourage self-regulation—a change in behavior.

The challenge in practicing EI is not in self-awareness. It lies in self-regulation. It can be relatively easy to recognize our strengths and somewhat simple to identify flaws. The test is in doing something about them—being able to draw upon the strengths enough to benefit from them yet not too much to misuse them. Then examining weaknesses to understand how they got there in the first place and realizing the importance of eliminating them to grow personally stronger.

In an effort to truly practice EI, the kaleidoscope leader believes the first step is desire. Without desire there is no victory in self-regulation. Within self-awareness individuals will confidently state their understanding of their faults and attributes. They will agree on the importance of modifying their behavior. But it stops there. Lacking in desire, they do not have the conviction to actually change.

Kaleidoscope leaders always have a desire to do more, be better, become stronger, and improve on their effectiveness. This constant longing to seize life, living from within focused on a notion of growth and change, is always first aligned with desire. The craving to constantly evolve is directly aligned with the highly emotionally intelligent—the kaleidoscope leader.

## Know Their Limitations

One common behavior in high-performing executives is their drive. They are known for their push for results, reaching goals on a regular basis and setting records of achievement. One thing that sets kaleidoscope leaders apart from others is, while on their quest for success, they know their limitations.

These individuals know when they are in over their heads and have the wherewithal to seek help. They realize when they don't have all the answers. They readily accept the fact that they don't possess all the knowledge. However, they know where to find it. This makes up a large part of the lifelong learning process.

One must know where to find the information they need. Whether it is in data sourced alone or through others, there must be a suppository to call on when needed. Today every leader uses the Internet to find things. Even the technologically unsophisticated can do a search. However, how many leaders have built a network of individuals they can call on for assistance? This is using the term *human resources* at its truest form. Along with using technology, every kaleidoscope leader surrounds themselves with people that possess talents and skills of all kinds, knowing when it is time to tap into them.

They also know when to quit. This is particularly hard for anyone that grew up in sports or continues to compete in activities outside of work. A constant message of never giving up can be devastating to sustained success. Emotionally intelligent leaders face the reality of areas they cannot overcome. They bring a halt to their current situation, assess next steps, realign, and move forward. Kaleidoscope leaders clearly know their limitations.

Practice Lifelong Learning

## Continue Striving for Excellence

When it is all said and done, kaleidoscope leaders continuously strive for excellence. They have a passion for being the best. They don't settle. They want to be at the top of the list and utilize their accomplishments for driving even greater results.

They thrive off exceeding expectations. They have the natural ability to examine what is required and then offer more. By finding ways to say yes, they easily overcome obstacles. They have the unique ability to turn problem resolution into loyalty. Whether it is a customer, employee, colleague, or vendor, kaleidoscope leaders use mistakes as a catalyst to create raving fans.

Their quality of work is above the rest. They encourage success in others by raising the bar and recognizing their little and big accomplishments. Through this desire to strive for excellence, they inspire others by collectively encouraging individual and team greatness.

They instinctively add value to all they do. Their need to exceed drives them to offer more and go the extra mile. With a limitless imagination, seeking to please comes easy. Going above and beyond is a way of life.

Striving for excellence and the kaleidoscope leader are synonymous.

# Tying the Leadership Style to the Kaleidoscope Belief

Now that you have read through Practice Lifelong Learning, let's examine how this belief affects the six styles of leadership.

## *The Solutions-Based Leader's Relationship to Practice Lifelong Learning*

### Tendencies:

- Well informed and stays current; is abreast of new ideas and methods that are designed to solve problems

- Uses staying up-to-date as a form of knowledgeable power

### Recommendations:

- Take more time contemplating the views of others versus making decisions in isolation

- Transition your quick decision making style to a more mindful approach by keeping your internal radar open

- Embrace limitations by surrounding yourself with those who have skills you do not possess
- Use a more collaborative manner in achieving excellence, steering away from leading with an individualistic approach

## *The Servant-Centered Leader's Relationship to Practice Lifelong Learning*

### Tendencies:

- Highly values individuality—learns from opposite views and opinions
- Easily identifies the strength in others when striving for excellence

### Recommendations:

- Take time for personal learning and growth versus always arranging development opportunities for others
- Don't hide behind the power of observation; be willing to make decisions with fewer facts
- Have a stronger willingness to hold others accountable for self-regulation
- Encourage others to stretch themselves as they

strive for excellence; don't accept average performance

## *The Process-Driven Leader's Relationship to Practice Lifelong Learning*

### Tendencies:

- Comfortable with seeking out new information, methods, and ideas in an effort to self-develop
- Utilizes the positive impact of understanding one's limitations

### Recommendations:

- Take time to gain knowledge outside of your immediate area of responsibility to become more open minded and well rounded
- Be more open to suggestions that are intuitive-based versus factual
- Recognize the value of opinions and sentiments along with facts and figures when seeking solutions
- Don't hide behind observation as means for more data when making decisions

Practice Lifelong Learning

## *The Financially-Focused Leader's Relationship to Practice Lifelong Learning*

### Tendencies:

- Open to learning trends and developments that impacts decisions
- Exhibits a great understanding of self-awareness and regulates easily when dealing within set parameters and goals

### Recommendations:

- Be willing to expand your knowledge beyond facts and figures
- Seek ideas and concepts that are more intuitive and different from your own
- Consider moods, feelings, and emotions when observing others
- Understand there is intangible excellence along with that you can measure

## *The Visionary Leader's Relationship to Practice Lifelong Learning*

### Tendencies:

- Embraces learning to guide innovative thinking
- Respects and welcomes thoughts contrary to their own

### Recommendations:

- Take time to learn concrete facts along with abstract information
- Contain emotions and be open to taking time to observe before making hasty decisions
- Realize when goals become too idealistic and impossible to accomplish
- Balance your desire for excellence with realistic outcomes

## *The Charismatic Leader's Relationship to Practice Lifelong Learning*

### Tendencies:

- Thoroughly enjoys and embraces learning information for business and pleasure

## Practice Lifelong Learning

- Capitalizes on the thoughts and ideas of others to generate even greater success

### Recommendations:

- Avoid becoming overly zealous in moving initiatives forward without taking time to consider feelings and emotions of others
- Seek to objectively self-assess opportunities for development
- Increase awareness of moving from optimism to realism when goals are unachievable
- Take time to share successes versus self-promotion

# Conclusion

Looking back, it is easy to see how kaleidoscope leaders operate. They have an unselfish approach to leading. They draw on their natural abilities of the six styles of leadership and are mindful of their shortcomings. They realize how each style is important and strengthens when the facets are comingled. As the kaleidoscope turns to offer ever-changing patterns, so does the kaleidoscope leader, shifting, adjusting, and altering to display the mannerisms necessary to help others achieve greatness.

Motivating, influencing, and stimulating individuals to be all that they can be becomes their main focus. By putting others first they lead based on a foundation of helping others succeed.

Caring drives the manner in which they contribute to others and the organization. This brings a deep commitment to taking responsibility for one's own actions, a realization of pointing the finger in versus out, as no one can be blamed for the kaleidoscope leader's actions but themselves.

This driving mind-set is fostered by their enthusiasm. Their positive approach becomes infectious, spreading an encouraging attitude to everyone it touches. Seeking a higher path is driven by desire and fueled by dedication to personal development and the growth of others.

By believing and knowing their success is predicated on the success of others, kaleidoscope leaders find their true mission in life.

www.ingramcontent.com/pod-product-compliance
Lightning Source LLC
Chambersburg PA
CBHW030842180526
45163CB00004B/1430